Ánimo 2

AQA

Self Study Guide

Isabel Alonso de Sudea

OXFORD
UNIVERSITY PRESS

OXFORD
UNIVERSITY PRESS

Great Clarendon Street, Oxford OX2 6DP

Oxford University Press is a department of the University of Oxford.
It furthers the University's objective of excellence in research, scholarship,
and education by publishing worldwide in

Oxford New York
Auckland Cape Town Dar es Salaam Hong Kong Karachi
Kuala Lumpur Madrid Melbourne Mexico City Nairobi
New Delhi Shanghai Taipei Toronto

With offices in

Argentina Austria Brazil Chile Czech Republic France Greece
Guatemala Hungary Italy Japan South Korea Poland Portugal
Singapore Switzerland Thailand Turkey Ukraine Vietnam

First published 2009

British Library Cataloguing in Publication Data

Data available

ISBN 978 019 915422 7

10 9 8 7 6 5 4 3 2 1

Typeset by PDQ Digital Media Solutions Ltd., Bungay, Suffolk

Printed in Great Britain by Ashford Colour Press Ltd.

Acknowledgements

The author and publisher would like to thank Imogen Fidler (editor) and
Ainara Solana (language consultant).

Contents

General Exam Tips

Here's a reminder of the topics from the AQA A2 specification which you need to revise for the examination. You have to study the first three topics and must also choose two cultural topics.

Environment

Pollution; Energy; Protecting the planet

Multicultural Society

Immigration; Integration; Racism

Contemporary Social Issues

Wealth and poverty; Law and order; Impact of scientific and technological progress

Cultural topics (two must be studied)

A region of Spain or of a Spanish-speaking country

A period of 20th century history in Spain or a Spanish-speaking country

The work of an author writing in Spanish

The work of a dramatist or poet writing in Spanish

The work of a director, architect, musician or painter from a Spanish-speaking community.

You will be taking two examinations:

Unit 3: Listening, Reading and Writing

This paper is worth 35% of your A Level and the time allowed is 2 hours 30 minutes.

There are three sections:

- Listening
- Reading and Writing
- Writing

Unit 4: Speaking Test

The Speaking Test is worth 15% of your A Level.

The test lasts 15 minutes and you have 20 minutes to prepare beforehand.

You are not allowed to use a dictionary.

There are two sections:

- Discussing a stimulus card (5 minutes)
- General conversation on topics you have studied (10 minutes).

Remember that your AS grade represents 50% of your A Level.

Pass grades for this examination range from A* and A down to E. The requirements are very similar to those for AS Level, but remember that this is in the context of the more demanding texts and tasks which you will meet at A2. Two new things which are expected are an ability to translate from and into Spanish accurately and an ability to cope with the unpredictable when you are talking to someone. Here's a reminder of the other expectations.

If you pass A Level Spanish with an A grade, it means you can:

- clearly understand the spoken language, including details and people's opinions.
- work out what someone is trying to say even if they don't spell it out in detail.
- clearly understand written texts, both the gist and the details.
- talk fluently, giving your opinions and justifying them, and using a good range of vocabulary and generally accurate pronunciation.
- organise your ideas and write them up well in Spanish.
- write using a wide range of vocabulary and grammatical structures without making many mistakes.

If you pass A Level Spanish with an E grade, it means you:

- show some understanding of spoken Spanish, even if you have difficulties when the language is complex and miss some of the details.
- can sometimes work out what someone is trying to say even if they don't give all the details.
- understand straightforward written texts, although you don't always understand more difficult writing.
- can talk in Spanish and convey basic information, perhaps a little hesitantly and relying on material you have learnt by heart. There is probably some English influence on your pronunciation.
- can convey information in writing, perhaps with some difficulty in organising your material and expressing it.
- use a range of vocabulary and structures, although quite often you make mistakes.

Preparing for the exams

You can see from these lists that when planning your revision there are really six areas you need to practise:

Speaking
Listening
Reading
Writing
Vocabulary
Grammar

There are tips on how to prepare each area on the page overleaf.

Speaking

- Take every opportunity to practise speaking Spanish – in lessons, with the language assistant, with a friend, with anyone you know who speaks Spanish.
- Think up some controversial statements linked to each topic from the first three sections on page 4 and practise arguing for or against them. An example would be *La cárcel no nos ayuda a reducir la tasa de criminalidad*. Record your ideas on tape and listen to see what areas still need practice – perhaps fluency, pronunciation or good use of vocabulary and structures.
- Think about all the aspects of the two cultural topics you have studied and practise explaining them and giving your opinions. Don't write everything out in full; note down a few key words for reference, but definitely no full sentences.

Listening

- Keep listening to Spanish, ideally every day. Use a mix of extracts you have worked on and new texts.
- Try listening to something for which you have the transcript. Just listen first, then listen again with the transcript and, if necessary, look up unknown words. Finally, listen again without the transcript and challenge yourself to understand everything.
- Watching films is excellent listening practice and watching more than once is even better! Try watching with the subtitles and then without. If you find this hard going, just re-watch a short extract.
- Spanish radio and TV programmes are useful, but can also be difficult. Record an extract and listen or watch it more than once. You will find it gets easier.
- Make sure you do some exam listening practice too!

Reading

- Keep reading a mix of things you read once quickly, such as a magazine, and things where you work hard at a short passage and try to understand everything. Texts from your textbook are useful for this.
- It's useful to note new vocabulary from your reading, but don't make it such hard work that you give up. Note, say, three new words from each text.
- Try a 'dual-language' reading book, where you get the original Spanish on one page and an English translation on the opposite one. This is an excellent way to practise reading longer texts without losing heart!
- Search on the Internet for articles in Spanish on any topic which interests you.

Writing

- Write out the basic facts for each aspect of the cultural topics you have studied and learn them.
- Practise planning essay questions on your cultural topics, jotting down ideas for each paragraph – in Spanish! – along with key vocabulary.
- Look carefully at marked work and identify what grammar errors you are making. Then check them in a grammar book and try some practice exercises.
- Make sure you are writing – and learning! – lists of key vocabulary for each of the two cultural topics. In addition, learn a good range of 'essay phrases' for introducing ideas, giving opinions, summing up and so on.

Vocabulary

- Learn lists of words regularly and make time to go back over words you learned a week or two ago. Reinforcement makes them stick!
- Choose a system of recording new words which works for you. It could be paper lists, small sections on individual cards, recording the words and their English meanings on tape, making posters to stick on your bedroom wall ... what's important is that you are noting the words and going over them regularly!
- You were probably encouraged to use a good range of vocabulary in the essays you wrote during the year. Go back over them, highlighting good words and phrases and writing the English in the margin, then use this to test yourself. Words are often easier to learn in context.

Grammar

- Keep doing practice exercises in areas where you know you are weak.
- Use reading texts to practise thinking grammatically. For example, highlight a selection of adjectives, then write out the English for the phrases in which they appear. Test yourself by reproducing the Spanish phrases accurately, complete with all the correct agreements!
- Keep learning from your verb tables until you know all the forms of each tense of regular verbs and the most common irregular verbs. Test yourself using a die: 1 = *yo*, 2 = *tú*, 3 = *él / ella / usted*, 4 = *nosotros*, 5 = *vosotros*, 6 = *ellos / ellas / ustedes*. Use a verb list, choose an infinitive and a tense at random, throw the die and say the correct form of the verb. Practise until you can do it without hesitation.

The Speaking Test: what you need to know

The test has two parts: discussing a stimulus card and a conversation on the two cultural topics you have studied.

Discussing a stimulus card (5 minutes)

Choose one of the two cards you are given and spend the preparation time on it.

- Decide which of the two views expressed on the card you are going to defend and prepare an outline of your reasons to last no more than one minute.
- The examiner will challenge you to defend your point of view. Try to predict what arguments s/he might use and then plan how you will counter them.
- You are allowed to make notes. Don't write out exactly what you will say, but do note some useful vocabulary for the topic and some expressions for voicing your opinion and for disagreeing with someone.

To do well on this section you need to develop a wide range of relevant arguments to defend the viewpoint you have chosen. You must respond readily to the examiner's arguments and be able to counter them robustly, giving reasons for your views and reasons why you don't accept that the points s/he makes are justified.

Conversation (10 minutes)

You will be asked to spend about five minutes discussing each of the cultural topics you have studied, i.e. two of the following:

- a region
- a historical period
- an author
- a poet or dramatist
- a director, architect, musician or painter.

This section is marked on three aspects:

- fluency, which means speaking confidently and sustaining a conversation at a natural pace.
- interaction, i.e. answering what you are asked, but also taking the opportunity to develop your ideas and coping if the examiner contradicts you.
- pronunciation and intonation, which really means sounding as 'Spanish' as possible.

In addition, **both** sections of the Speaking Test are marked for knowledge of grammar. You need to use a variety of structures and a good range of vocabulary, without making too many errors!

Card A – Energía

- Look at the card and read the two statements in the speech bubbles.
- Choose **one** and think how you can convey and expand on its main ideas.
- Begin the discussion by outlining your point of view (this should take no more than one minute).
- You must then be prepared to respond to anything the examiner might say and to justify your point of view.
- You may be required to explain something you have said, to respond to an opposing point of view expressed by the examiner, or to defend your expressed opinion(s).
- You may make notes in your preparation time and refer to them during this part of the examination.

¿Cómo conseguir la energía en el futuro?

Es imprescindible desarrollar otras formas de energía para el futuro. Dentro de poco, las fuentes tradicionales se agotarán y habrá que encontrar otros recursos que sean renovables.

La mejor solución son las centrales nucleares. Ante todo, la industria atómica es limpia y eficaz y nos proporcionará hoy y en el futuro una energía por unidad de masa millones de veces superior a las demás fuentes de energía.

This is **not** an exercise which requires you to balance both sides of an argument. Decide which of the two points of view you are going to defend, then stick to it! Come up with several reasons which support this viewpoint and be prepared to express them concisely in the opening section of the discussion.

Whichever side of the argument you choose to defend, the examiner will come up with reasons to challenge you. Prepare for this by writing a list of arguments s/he might use, then working out what you will say to counter each one. Look back at the speaking card on page 9, decide which side of the argument you are going to defend and write a list of tricky questions the examiner might ask you. When you have done that, work out a good answer for each one. Then compare your ideas with those given upside down below.

A favor de la energía renovable

¿Usted no cree que es poco realista pensar que se puede producir toda la energía necesaria en el futuro mediante las energías renovables?
Pues en la actualidad posiblemente no sea del todo realista pero estoy convencido de que debemos seguir buscando e investigando nuevos métodos y a la larga creo que será posible, sobre todo empleando una variedad de recursos. En mi opinión, es importante disponer de diversas fuentes de recursos.

Piense un poco en el transporte. La energía eólica jamás podrá reemplazar el petróleo, por ejemplo.
No estoy tan seguro. Si siempre hubiéramos pensado así no habríamos continuado investigando los coches eléctricos ni el biodiésel. Es precisamente buscando soluciones alternativas como los científicos encuentran algo poco usual que sirve.

No cabe duda alguna que si el consumo sigue al paso de hoy en día no habrá suficiente energía en el futuro sobre todo si dependemos de la energía removable.
Exacto. Hace falta determinación política para resolver la crisis energética. Además, todos malgastamos energía y cada cual debe tomar responsabilidad y aprender a limitar su uso; por ejemplo ...

A favor de la energía nuclear

En primer lugar hay que aceptar que la energía nuclear es peligrosa y corremos el riesgo de otro Chernóbil ¿verdad?
Está bien – no se puede negar lo de Chernóbil y siempre hay que tenerlo en mente, pero creo que hoy en día comprendemos más y sabemos manejar la energía nuclear mejor que hace veinte años.

En segundo lugar, la industria atómica no ha sabido solucionar el problema de cómo ni dónde almacenar los residuos radioactivos –¿no es así?
Hasta cierto punto tiene usted razón. Es un asunto problemático pero ya hay varios países donde se está buscando una solución a este problema y no cabe duda de que está en su propio interés encontrarla ...

¿Y qué me dice del riesgo de que se produzca un ataque terrorista en una central?
Pues hay que tener en cuenta que las amenazas están presentes cada día en todo lo que hacemos. Tanto en las centrales como en muchos otros aspectos de la vida es importante protegernos contra estos problemas ...

Card B – Integration

- Look at the card and read the two statements in the speech bubbles.
- Choose **one** and think how you can convey and expand on its main ideas.
- Begin the discussion by outlining your point of view (this should take no more than one minute).
- You must then be prepared to respond to anything the examiner might say and to justify your point of view.
- You may be required to explain something you have said, to respond to an opposing point of view expressed by the examiner, or to defend your expressed opinion(s).
- You may make notes in your preparation time and refer to them during this part of the examination.

¿La integración social es un sueño imposible?

Claro que sí porque las diferencias de nivel económico y de cultura, raza o lengua solamente acrecientan las divisiones obvias en la sociedad.

Hay que reconocer que la integración social es un proceso lento, pero poco a poco la gente aprende a tolerar y a respetar a los demás y se da cuenta de que la diversidad enriquece su país.

Read and listen to a section of this student's Speaking Test based on Card B. It is the part where the examiner begins to challenge his views (track 2).

Las divisiones sociales siempre han existido y siempre existirán ¿verdad?

Claro que existen diferencias culturales y de costumbres. Siempre ha habido diferentes lenguas, idiomas y creencias, pero una sociedad civilizada fomenta la tolerancia y el respeto y es precisamente esto lo que sirve para consolidar y fortalecer la cohesión social. Tenemos muchos ejemplos de ello. Son los políticos los que muchas veces no quieren comprender o prefieren dividir a la gente por sus ansias de poder y riqueza.

No se puede negar que muchas veces son las diferencias de riqueza las que dividen a la sociedad y causan problemas.

No cabe duda y es evidente en todas las sociedades del mundo, pero esto no quiere decir que sea una barrera a la integración. Al contrario, los que tienen más tienen una responsabilidad hacia los que tienen menos. Lo que pasa con el sistema de comercio libre es que la avaricia y el egoísmo prevalecen. Los sistemas de impuestos son un ejemplo que demuestra hasta qué punto queremos ayudar a los menos favorecidos de nuestra sociedad.

¿Qué me dice de los grupos que no se quieren integrar en la sociedad y se automarginan?

No creo que tenga usted razón cuando dice que no quieren integrarse. Lo que pasa es que se sienten marginados y rechazados porque saben que no van a ser aceptados o porque perciben actitudes xenófobas producto de discursos populistas. A veces se juntan por miedo a lo desconocido pero cuando llegan a familiarizarse con la comunidad donde viven las cosas cambian para bien.

Es un poco ingenuo pensar que la víctima de un crimen vaya a abrazar a un chaval que le ha robado o hasta causado daño físico ¿no le parece?

Me parece que la prensa popular es la responsable de ciertos prejuicios que tenemos respecto a este tema. Hay que tener en cuenta que el comportamiento antisocial es a menudo el producto de las diferencias sociales. A mi modo de ver siempre es mucho mejor tratar de reintegrar a una persona y reeducarla para que pueda participar en la sociedad de una manera positiva. Los castigos sólo sirven para que siga siendo una fuente de conflicto en la sociedad en que vive.

Bueno, ahora me gustaría saber por qué ...

Learn some useful phrases for disagreeing (politely!) with the examiner. Examples include:

No creo; al contrario; yo creo que ...
No estoy de acuerdo con usted en absoluto, porque ...
En mi opinión usted no tiene razón / usted se equivoca porque ...
Pues, yo diría que ...
Posiblemente sí, pero no hay que olvidarse de que ...

Write out plenty of key facts for each of your two topics and learn them thoroughly. You won't be asked to recite them, but you will be able to slip them in as examples to illustrate the points you are making. Knowing your material really well will give you the confidence to speak fluently.

Here are some practice questions for each kind of topic. Listen to 10 students answering sample questions on the CD (track 3). You'll find the transcripts in a Microsoft Word® document on the CD.

A region

- ¿Qué aspectos de la geografía de esta región o este país le interesan?
- ¿Cuál ha sido el período histórico más interesante en esta región o este país? ¿Por qué?
- ¿Cuáles son las industrias más importantes de esta región o este país?
- ¿Es una región o un país más bien rico o pobre?
- ¿Se puede hablar de un habitante 'típico' de este país o esta región?
- ¿Ha habido cambios demográficos en este país o esta región?
- ¿El turismo desempeña un papel importante?
- ¿Le gustaría trabajar o vivir en este país o esta región?

A historical period

- Describa los acontecimientos más importantes del período.
- ¿Cuál ha sido la causa principal de estos acontecimientos?
- ¿Qué influencia tuvieron sobre la época?
- ¿Todavía influyen hoy en día? ¿Cómo?
- Hable de una persona importante de esta época y la influencia que tenía.
- ¿Cómo juzga usted las ideas de la época?
- ¿Le hubiera gustado vivir durante esta época? ¿Por qué sí / no?

A person (author / poet / director / etc.)

- Describa las influencias culturales que recibió este autor / poeta / dramaturgo / director / arquitecto / músico / pintor.
- ¿Cuáles son los temas principales y cómo los expresa en sus obras?
- ¿Qué libro (obra de teatro / pintura etc.) admira usted más y por qué?
- ¿Hay algunos aspectos que no le gustan tanto de sus obras? ¿Cuáles son? ¿Por qué?
- ¿Cómo ha influido su vida en sus obras?
- En su opinión, ¿los jóvenes aprecian mucho a este arquitecto (dramaturgo / pintor etc.)? ¿Por qué?
- Explique por qué le gustan a usted las obras de este autor (director etc.).

Remember that the conversation will not be confined to the merely factual. In addition to conveying what you have learned about the topic, you need to be able to discuss it. That might mean speculating about causes and effects, giving your opinions and justifying them, or predicting how things might develop in the future. Think about the ideas you will want to express and the language which is suitable for conveying them.

You can plan your time as you wish, but it is suggested that you allocate it roughly as follows:

- Half an hour for the listening questions in Section A
- An hour for the reading and writing questions in Section A
- An hour for the essay question in Section B.

Section A: Listening, Reading and Writing (70 marks)

Listening

There will be about five minutes of recording altogether and you will be able to play it, replay it and pause it yourself. There will be four passages with various types of question in Spanish, for example:

- finding errors in summary statements and correcting them
- matching sentence halves
- ticking those statements which are true
- sentence beginnings with multiple choice endings.

Reading and Writing

First, there will be three different types of questions in Spanish, such as:

- choosing words from a box to complete gaps in the text
- reading a number of texts, then matching summary sentences to them
- reading a text and marking statements about it as 'V' (*verdad*), 'F' (*falso*) or 'N' (*no se menciona*).

Then there will be two translation questions:

- translating a short passage of Spanish into English
- translating English sentences into Spanish.

Section B: Writing on Cultural Topics

You have to write **one** essay of **at least** 250 words on **one** of the two cultural topics you have studied. There will be a choice of four essay questions, two on each topic.

The key ways to prepare are by:

- doing plenty of listening practice to keep your ear 'tuned in' to Spanish
- reading a wide variety of materials linked to the topics listed on page 4
- practising writing 250-word essays on cultural topics in about one hour
- working through the exam-type questions and tips on the following pages.

Listening task 1 – Llegó la super-abuela (Track 4)

Todas las frases de abajo contienen un error. Escucha el reportaje y en cada frase tacha el error y corrígelo como en el ejemplo.

Ejemplo
Hacen falta ~~guardianes~~ niños pequeños en España. *guarderías*

a) España ha contado unos 1,5 millones de niños menores de tres años.

b) Poco más de la mitad asisten a una guardería privada o del estado.

c) Normalmente son los abuelos los que cuidan a los niños en casa.

d) Los abuelos ya pueden gozar de su jubilación.

There are usually two or three details in a sentence which could be wrong. For c), it could be any of the details marked here in bold:

Normalmente *son* ***los abuelos*** *los que* ***cuidan*** *a los niños en casa.*

But listen carefully and you will realise that *normalmente* means more or less the same as *suelen ser*. Also, *cuidan* is an appropriate verb because the report is about caring for children. But *abuelos* is not accurate, because the text makes it clear that it is specifically the *abuelas* who do most of the caring, although *abuelos* are mentioned.

Al igual que ocurre en muchos países del mundo, en España no hay suficientes guarderías para niños menores de tres años. Se supone que la familia cuida de ellos y no el estado. Pero hoy en día España cuenta con 1,5 millones de niños de esta edad y sólo el 45% tiene un puesto en una guardería, sea del estado o privada. Los demás no tienen más remedio que quedarse con un miembro de la familia – y este miembro suele ser la abuela.

Las abuelas pueden olvidarse de la jubilación y el descanso merecidos a los sesenta y pico años. Un reportaje dice que hasta el 70% de mujeres españolas de más de 65 años de edad cuida a sus nietos y el 22% lo hace a diario. Además cabe mencionar que los abuelos pasan por lo menos 20 horas por semana con sus nietos.

Por fin el gobierno ha reconocido estos hechos y ha decidido invertir aproximadamente 1,5 billones de euros para mejorar el cuidado de los peques y la vida de los pensionistas.

Listening task 2 – Zaragoza: sede de la Expo (Track 5)

Escucha este reportaje sobre la expo de Zaragoza. Completa cada casilla con la letra correcta. ¡Cuidado! Sobran tres expresiones.

a) a lo que se parece [C]

b) para lo que sirve [A]

c) lo que significa [ ]

d) lo que pone en el punto de mira [ ]

e) lo que va a celebrarse [ ]

A un pretexto para transformar la ciudad
B una grandiosa muestra
C la Expo de Sevilla
D celebrar una exposición
E impulsar el desarrollo urbanístico
F la gran fiesta del agua
G la capital aragonesa
H terminar los pabellones

Read the questions really carefully. Here, questions b) and c) look rather similar, but one is asking what the purpose is and the other what the meaning is. Remember too, that questions like this usually follow the order in which the answers are mentioned in the passage. Consider both these factors and you should be able to pick out the key parts of the recording which refer to each question. For question a), it's *la Expo de Sevilla*. For question e), it's trickier because you hear the word *celebrar* in the middle section of the recording in relation to the *exposiciones* but then in the final section the word *celebración* gives you the lead into *la … fiesta del agua* which is the answer required.

De nuevo España es sede de una grandiosa muestra parecida a la Exposición Universal de 1992 en Sevilla. Es sin lugar a dudas un pretexto para transformar la ciudad y sus alrededores e impulsar su desarrollo urbanístico, económico, cultural y por supuesto turístico hacia nuevos horizontes.

Este parece ser el doble sentido de todas las exposiciones universales e internacionales que se celebran cada año en el mundo entero y por las que pujan siempre ciudades de los cinco continentes.

Zaragoza ganó la contienda y ahora este es su año. Bajo el título 'Agua y Desarrollo Sostenible' la ciudad inauguró su exposición, que pondrá a la capital aragonesa en el punto de mira del mundo. Ya con los pabellones y edificios vanguardistas terminados, el casco antiguo y el resto de la ciudad renuevan sus espacios, zonas verdes e infraestructuras, y comienza la celebración de la gran fiesta del agua, siempre abrazada por el Ebro, río entrañable del norte del país.

Listening task 3 – La esperanza sale a flote (Track 6)

Escucha este ejemplo de ayuda humanitaria. Indica mediante un ✓ las **cinco** frases verdaderas.

a) Se trata de un doctor de medicina tropical. ☐

b) Vive en una región extraña de la selva amazónica. ☐

c) No se puede entrar allí sin que lo autoricen los indios. ☐

d) Las comunidades solían excluir a los que sufrían enfermedades. ☐

e) Hay mucha incidencia de esta enfermedad contagiosa allí. ☐

f) Su consultorio está dentro de un barco que va por el río. ☐

g) Busca la sanidad de los agentes. ☐

h) La gente local enseña medicina. ☐

i) Trata de curar a los indígenas actuando a tiempo. ☐

j) Trata de crear líderes para que se curen a sí mismos. ☐

You need to understand small details to work out whether the statements mean the same as the recording. For example, you must be able to distinguish between the word *extraña* in statement b) and *extranjeros* in the text to avoid being tricked into thinking the statement is correct. Similarly, for c), realising that there is a connection between *sin que lo autoricen* and *con la autorización* will help you reach the right decision.

Se trata de una doctora de Extremadura que lucha contra la lepra en la parte más remota de la Amazonia brasileña.

La doctora López, especializada en medicina tropical, es una de los pocos extranjeros que viven en esta parte aislada del mundo. A este lugar solo se puede llegar en taxi aéreo y con la autorización de la Fundación Nacional del Indio (FUNAI). Hace ya años fue el lugar donde escondieron a los leprosos que, excluidos de sus comunidades buscaban refugio donde fuera. Actualmente, es la segunda zona del mundo con mayor incidencia de esta enfermedad contagiosa después de la India.

Bueno pues es aquí donde trabaja nuestra doctora pasando consulta por las aldeas a bordo de un hospital fluvial – un barco adaptado que pasea por el río. Trata de formar agentes sanitarios entre la población local y enseña medicina preventiva contra múltiples enfermedades. Lo bueno es que si se actúa con tiempo y con tratamientos todos los pacientes se curan.

Lo más conveniente es darles las herramientas que están pidiendo para que puedan liderar sus propios proyectos. Las poblaciones indígenas son grandes conservacionistas. Enseñan a cuidar la naturaleza y sus conocimientos de las plantas son valiosísimas para Occidente.

Listening task 4 – Soldados humanitarios (Track 7)

Escucha este reportaje sobre unos niños. Selecciona la opción A, B o C para completar las frases. Escribe A, B o C en cada casilla.

a) El Ejército del Aire español ... [ ]

A evacuó a los niños de Irak

B describió un viaje a los niños de Irak

C facilitó la llegada de los niños de Irak

b) Los niños lograron ... [ ]

A descubrir un mundo diferente

B ver el paisaje alrededor de Sevilla

C traumatizar a sus monitores

c) Pasaron el tiempo ... [ ]

A realizando una variedad de actividades

B siguiendo clases de religión

C recordando la guerra

Here, you are being asked to sum up quite long sections of the text by choosing the most appropriate answer. When you read the transcript, notice that the whole of the first paragraph conveys the answer to question a), i.e. the involvement of the Spanish Air Force. Similarly, only one of the alternatives for questions b) and c) sums up accurately what the children did.

¡Es un sueño hecho realidad!

Así describen su viaje a España unos 56 niños iraquíes, llevados a un campamento de verano en la base aérea de Armilla, Granada. Llegaron gracias al Ejército del Aire español. Cuando sus monitores les llevaron de visita al Parque Temático de Isla Mágica en Sevilla preguntaron encantados si eso era el paraíso.

Port supuesto esto es lo que les parecía porque han logrado dejar atrás el paisaje traumático de la posguerra iraquí y han descubierto una cultura y una realidad hasta ahora inimaginables para ellos.

"Hemos aprendido muchas cosas, pero lo que más nos ha gustado es el orden que hay aquí, lo bien que nos han tratado, los juegos, los sitios y los edificios que hemos visto" explica uno de los niños.

Las excursiones se alternaron con clases con sus profesores habituales, venidos desde Irak, y con sus mismas tradiciones religiosas y gastronómicas.

La sombra de la guerra de Irak no ha tenido apenas cabida en este lugar seguro, gracias a las labores humanitarias que desempeña el ejército español.

Reading task 1 – Marcha en contra de las bases de Rota

Rellena los espacios de este texto con una de las palabras de la lista. ¡Cuidado! Sobran dos palabras.

Ayer acudieron unas 2.000 (a) .... a la XXII Marcha a Rota para reclamar el desmantelamiento de las (b) .... norteamericanas en este municipio gaditano y en Morón de la Frontera. Además bajo el (c) .... 'Ninguna vida más, ningún (d) .... más, ninguna guerra, nunca más' los (e) .... pidieron la retirada de las (f) .... españolas de Afganistán.

El coordinador general Diego Valderas explicó que se había cumplido el objetivo de la marcha, en la que las (g) .... participantes, como Ecologistas en Acción entre muchas otras, se han situado en el liderazgo de las asociaciones que luchan por la (h) .... y la solidaridad y que, con una mayor nitidez, luchan contra el (i) .... estadounidense para aspirar a que en un (j) .... determinado, las bases de Rota y Morón de la Frontera dejen de estar en nuestro territorio como plataformas de Guerra, de miseria y de explotación al servicio de los Estados Unidos de América.

aviones	lema	imperialismo	soldado
personas	país	bases	formaciones
tiempo	paz	manifestantes	tropas

Always start with the words you are most sure of. Where you are not sure, it helps to remember that each word must fit grammatically into its gap – for example, should it be masculine or feminine, singular or plural? Check each of the determiners (articles or adjectives) which give a clue as to which type is required: there are four gaps in this text which have feminine plural determiners in front of them and will therefore need a feminine plural noun: *unas* (a), *las* (b), *las* (f), *las* (g). When you have placed as many words as you can, finally decide which ones don't fit or make sense anywhere.

Reading task 2 – La Duquesa Roja

Lee este artículo. Para cada frase indica si es verdadera (V), falsa (F)or no se menciona (N).

Luisa, Duquesa de Medina Sidonia, quien a la edad de setenta un años murió de una pulmonía, es recordada con respeto y afecto en España como la mujer que desafió al dictador Francisco Franco. En 1966 no hizo caso de la censura de la prensa y anunció al mundo que cerca de Palomares, un pueblo en la costa de Almería, se habían extraviado cuatro bombas nucleares.

Todo sucedió el 17 de enero de ese año, cuando un bombardero B-52 de las Fuerzas Aéreas Americanas chocó con otro avión americano causando el accidente nuclear más grave de la guerra fría. Explosivos convencionales en dos de las bombas se explotaron esparciendo radiación; otras tres bombas fueron rescatadas pero una cuarta que cayó al mar no fue encontrada hasta unos tres meses más tarde.

La Duquesa aprovechó su título para hacer llegar la noticia a la prensa mundial y pidió compensación para el pueblo almeriense. Después de varias manifestaciones fue arrestada y la dictadura pidió su silencio. Se negó a callar y pasó ocho meses de cárcel en Alcalá. Al salir de allí escribió un libro testimonio de las condiciones miserables en prisión y otro sobre el caso de Palomares. Fue censurado y no llegó a publicarse hasta 2002.

a) Fue la única mujer que criticó al dictador Francisco Franco. ☐

b) El gobierno español impuso un bloqueo informativo sobre el accidente. ☐

c) Dos aviones explotaron sobre la costa almeriense. ☐

d) La contaminación radioactiva fue muy peligrosa. ☐

e) La Duquesa no quiso que la noticia llegara a la prensa mundial. ☐

f) Prefirió ser encarcelada a tener que callar sobre lo que había pasado. ☐

Be careful to base your assessment of the statements on what it says in the text and not on things you know or believe to be true. The answer to statement d) looks likely to be 'V', because it reports a fact we know is true of radioactive materials generally but because there is no mention of 'contaminación' in the passage you need to mark it 'N'.

Here again your knowledge of synonyms will help you. Linking *un bloqueo informativo* to *la censura de la prensa* will help you get question b) right.

Reading and Writing task 3 – El fenómeno del niño

Traduce al inglés este texto.

Con 23 años, Mark Zuckerberg se ha convertido en uno de los personajes más influyentes del mundo gracias a la creación de Facebook. La red ya cuenta con más de sesenta y cuatro millones de usuarios que comparten sus opiniones y gustos con sus amigos. ¿Quién fue ese genio que, cuando tenía apenas diecinueve años, creó este monstruo de la Internet?

Ya en su segundo año en Harvard casi se gana una expulsión por sus travesuras como hacker. Creó Facesmash, una página en la que los alumnos universitarios podían formar parejas y votar por los más atractivos del plantel. Fue un éxito total. Desde entonces se obsesionó con la idea de crear una red social.

Beware of 'false friends' or words which look like English words, but mean something different. Think carefully about the translation of words such as 'personajes' and 'usuarios'.

Remember that a literal translation will not always sound right in English. What expression would be better than 'when he hardly had 19 years' for *cuando tenía apenas diecinueve años*? What phrase and tense will you use to translate *casi se gana una expulsión*?

Where possible, keep your English translation closely in line with the Spanish because doing so cuts down the risk of missing out parts of the sentence. But sometimes the English version will sound more natural if you alter the word order a little or rephrase something. This has been done in the suggested translation of the final paragraph of the text: compare the two versions carefully.

At 23 years old, Mark Z has ~~become~~ transformed into one of the most influential people of the world. Thanks to the creation of Facebook. The network already has more than 64 million users who share their opinions and likes / ~~tastes~~ with their friends. ¿ Who was that genius that, when he was hardly 19, created this Internet Monster?

Already in his 2nd year at Harvard, he almost got expelled for his reputation as a hacker. He created facesmash, a page where uni students could create pairs and vote for the most attractive one. It was a massive success. Since then, he was obsessed with the idea to create a social network

Reading and Writing task 4

Traduce las frases siguientes al español.

a) After months of very little rain Catalonia has had to ask Madrid for help.

b) However, it's doubtful they will be able to resolve the problem quickly.

c) The country is struggling to deal with the worst drought in forty years.

d) Catalonia, in the north-east, has been severely affected.

e) Authorities in Barcelona are going to fine people for watering the garden.

f) No one is allowed to fill a swimming pool of more than 300 square metres.

g) Fountains have been emptied and beach showers turned off.

Think grammatically! Which sentence or sentences require you to use each of the following? Work it out, then check the answers, which are printed upside down.

- **i** the present continuous tense
- **ii** a verb which is followed by 'por'
- **iii** a phrase followed by the subjunctive
- **iv** an infinitive where English uses the '-ing' form of the verb
- **v** a negative construction
- **vi** a superlative
- **vi** a verb in the passive
- **viii** a verb in the perfect tense
- **ix** a definite article where you don't need one in English

i c; **ii** c, e; **iii** b; **iv** e; **v** f; **vi** c; **vii** g; **viii** a, d and g; **ix** e

Check the grammar of your finished translations very carefully. Is every verb in the correct tense and does it agree with its subject? Does every adjective agree with the noun it describes?

You have to write an essay of at least 250 words on one of the cultural topics studied. The three vital stages are planning, writing and checking.

Planning

Don't rush this stage: five or ten minutes thinking about the question, deciding on your argument and dividing it into paragraphs, jotting down the facts you want to use and thinking out a good introduction and conclusion is time very well spent. Keep referring back to the title to make sure every paragraph is relevant to the question. You might also note vocabulary and phrases you want to use in each paragraph. Then, when everything is in order, start writing, and stick to your plan!

Writing

Work through your notes for each paragraph. Write them up using a variety of sentence lengths, interesting vocabulary and a range of grammatical constructions. Be especially careful about the links between the paragraphs, so the examiner can follow the argument easily. A phrase like *A continuación hay que decir que ...* can introduce ideas which build on those in the previous paragraph, but if you want to move on to a different angle you might start with *En cambio ...* or *Sin embargo es necesario decir también que ...*

It helps if you write on alternate lines. This will make it easier for you to spot mistakes when checking through your work and also allows you space to write in any corrections.

Checking

Read your essay once through to check the flow of ideas and make sure each sentence makes sense. Then do a more detailed check, looking especially for these common errors:

- verbs which don't agree with their subject or are in the wrong tense
- adjectives which don't match the noun they describe
- phrases which are not idiomatic and don't sound Spanish
- misspellings, especially of words similar to, but not the same as, English ones
- missing accents

The marks for this question are awarded as follows:

- **Content: 25 marks**
  i.e. a thorough understanding of the topic, with relevant examples and well justified opinions and a well structured, logical argument.

- **Vocabulary: 5 marks**
  i.e. a wide range of topic-specific words and good 'essay phrases'.

- **Use of complex structures: 5 marks**
  i.e. including a range of tenses, the subjunctive, conjunctions, phrases such as *después de haber* + past participle, *al* + infinitive, and so on.

- **Accuracy: 5 marks**

Grammar Summary

All the grammar you learned for AS is still needed and there are some extra points for A2. Pages 25-31 revise AS grammar, reminding you what you should know and giving you phrases and sentences to translate into Spanish for practice. Pages 32-33 revise the points you will be learning on the A2 course, also practised through sentences to translate.

Grammar is even more important at A2 than it was at AS. So, what can you do to make sure you really do know your stuff?

Pay attention when grammar is explained! If you learn the rules and their exceptions and do some practice exercises, you will be surprised how much of it will stick.

Accept that there is quite a lot of detail to master and be prepared to go over things regularly. Re-read your grammar notes, re-do practice exercises, ask questions if you come across things you don't fully understand.

Be pro-active. Go through marked written work, looking carefully at the things which have been corrected. Decide which ones are 'silly mistakes' caused by forgetting things which you know well, and make a list of them so you can try to avoid them in the future. Then look for errors where you are not quite sure what is wrong. Ask, if necessary, then look that grammar point up in the grammar section of your textbook and in the relevant section of the grammar workbook. Keep practising and asking questions until you do understand it. When you understand it, review it by writing grammar notes on it in your own words, adding examples.

Make a list of example sentences from your written work which use some of the more complex grammar points well. Learn them, and use them as models for other sentences with different vocabulary but using the same basic structure. Make a point of including a good variety of grammatical structures in the practice essays you write.

Work through the exercises on the following pages. If there are practice sentences you find hard to translate, learn the correct version from the answer section by heart.

Revision of AS Grammar: nouns, determiners, adjectives, adverbs

Check the grammar section of Ánimo 2 and/or the Grammar Workbook if you need to know more about any of these areas:

- typical masculine endings for nouns, such as *-o, -e, -l, -r, -u, -y* and exceptions
- typical feminine endings for nouns, such as *-a, -ión, -ad, -ed* and exceptions
- forming plural nouns and adjectives; vowel + *s*; consonant + *es*; *z* ⟶ *ces*
- when to use and when not to use the definite and indefinite articles
- how and when to shorten adjectives like *grande* ⟶ *gran; bueno* ⟶ *buen* etc.
- how the position of an adjective can change its meaning: *un gran hombre / un hombre grande*
- forming possessive adjectives like *mi, tu, su, nuestro/a/os/as; vuestro/a/os/as; sus*
- forming adverbs using the feminine form of the adjective plus *-mente* and irregular adverbs like *bien* and *mal.*
- using *más, menos* and *tan / como* to form comparisons and *el más* or *el menos* to form superlatives
- using irregular comparisons like *mejor / peor / menor / mayor* or irregular superlatives like *el mejor / el peor*

Translate into Spanish:

1 Milk is healthier than coffee.
2 Salt is not good for you either.
3 You should drink water every day.
4 Lights in town are brighter than they used to be.
5 My mother is a nurse and my bother is a journalist.
6 Her dream is to be a great tennis player.
7 Spanish wine is just as good as French wine.
8 Our house uses less energy now than before.
9 That is the worst picture you have painted.
10 You are the third man to ask me that question.

1 La leche es más saludable que el café.
2 La sal tampoco es buena.
3 Deberías beber agua todos los días.
4 Las luces de la ciudad son más brillantes que antes.
5 Mi madre es enfermera y mi hermano es periodista.
6 Su sueño es ser un gran tenista.
7 El vino español es tan bueno como el vino francés.
8 Nuestra casa usa menos energía ahora que antes.
9 Ese es el peor cuadro que has pintado.
10 Usted es el tercer hombre que me ha hecho esa pregunta.

Revision of AS Grammar: pronouns

Check the grammar section of Ánimo 2 and/or the Grammar Workbook if you need to know more about any of these areas:

- personal pronouns: *tú / vosotros; usted / ustedes*
- direct object pronouns: *me, te, lo, la, nos, os, los, las*
- indirect object pronouns: *me, te, le, nos, os, les*
- emphatic pronouns, used after prepositions: *para mi, ti, él, ella, nosotros, vosotros, ellos, ellas*
- reflexive pronouns, used with reflexive verbs: *me, te, se, nos, os, se*
- the position of pronouns in a sentence, especially when there is more than one: *me los dio; dámelos ahora; ¿Cuándo vas a levantarte? Ya se ha levantado.*
- when two third person object pronouns come together change the first one to *se*
- the relative pronoun *que*, which you can never leave out as you can in English
- other relative pronouns: *de quien / quienes; el que / el cual; donde*
- possessive pronouns: *el mío / la mía / los míos / las mías etc.; el tuyo, el suyo, el nuestro, el vuestro, los suyos*, which agree in gender and number with the noun they modify
- demonstrative adjectives and pronouns: *este / esta / estos / estas*
- indefinite pronouns and adjectives: *alguno (algún) / alguna / algunos / algunas*

Translate into Spanish

1 Explain to me what you want from me.
2 Which of these two presents do you prefer?
3 These shirts are the best. I don't like those.
4 Someone loves you but I'm not sure who!
5 That's her book so give it to her now please.
6 Here's some chocolate. Eat it all up – it won't make you fat.
7 These are my glasses. Where are yours?
8 I prefer to sit by the fire in winter. What about you?
9 Whose is this CD? Is it hers or his?
10 Neither. I think it must be ours.

1 Explícame lo que quieres de mí.
2 ¿Cuál de estos dos regalos prefieres?
3 Estas camisas son las mejores. No me gustan aquéllas.
4 ¡Alguien te quiere pero no estoy seguro de quién!
5 Ese es su libro, así que dáselo ahora, por favor.
6 Aquí tienes chocolate. Cómetelo todo – no te engordará.
7 Estas son mis gafas. ¿Dónde están las tuyas?
8 Prefiero sentarme al lado de la chimenea en invierno. ¿Y tú?
9 ¿De quién es este CD? ¿Es de ella o de él?
10 Ninguno de los dos. Creo que debe de ser nuestro.

Revision of AS Grammar: infinitives, the simple present and present continuous tenses, impersonal and third person verbs

Check the grammar section of Ánimo 2 and/or the Grammar Workbook if you need to know more about any of these areas:

- the use of the infinitive as a noun, in instructions or in two-verb constructions e.g. *sonreír es bueno; no pisar el cesped; ¿Me permite fumar? hacer venir*
- the infinitive as used after verbs followed by the prepositions *a* and *de*, such as *ayudar a, tratar de, volver a, acabar de*
- the present tense of regular and radical changing verbs, such as *hablar, comer, vivir; jugar (ue), empezar (ie), dormir (ue), pedir (i)* and where the spelling changes occur
- the present tense of the modal verbs *querer, deber* and *poder*
- the present tense of irregular verbs such as *ir, tener, hacer*, and the different usages of *ser* and *estar* plus many less common irregular verbs
- the present participle and the present continuous; *-ando; -iendo*; *estoy leyendo; está durmiendo*
- the use of the present tense with *desde (hace)*
- the passive form of the present tense in sentences like *su beca es pagada por el gobierno*
- the use of *gustar* and other third person and impersonal verbs; *me interesa; no se puede entrar*

Translate into Spanish

1 I always make it clear that I don't like racism.
2 We try to help people to understand the issues.
3 Tolerance plays an important part in social integration.
4 Children play together without a problem.
5 We must work hard to prevent local crime.
6 Why are such stupid laws allowed to be passed?
7 He has been organising political campaigns for years.
8 It's good to take part in charity walks.
9 They are looking for other ways to support the cause.
10 I am delighted to work for this charity.

1 Siempre dejo claro que no me gusta el racismo.
2 Tratamos de ayudar a la gente a comprender los asuntos.
3 La tolerancia desempeña un papel importante en la cohesión social.
4 Los niños juegan juntos sin problema.
5 Debemos trabajar duro para prevenir el crimen local.
6 ¿Por qué se permite que se aprueben leyes tan estúpidas?
7 Hace años que organiza campañas políticas.
8 Es bueno participar en caminatas benéficas.
9 Están buscando otras maneras de apoyar la causa.
10 Me encanta trabajar para esta ONG.

Revision of AS Grammar: future and conditional tenses plus negatives

Check the grammar section of Ánimo 2 and/or the Grammar Workbook if you need to know more about any of these areas:

- using the present tense to refer to things which are going to happen soon, especially if a future time is mentioned: *voy a casa de mi amiga esta noche; ¿por qué no vemos este programa mañana?*
- using *ir* + infinitive to say what is going to happen in the near future: *voy a llegar tarde esta noche; vamos a bailar el sábado por la noche*
- using *me gustaría; tengo la intención de; pienso* etc. + an infinitive to refer to future plans which are not certain: *me gustaría viajar por el mundo algún día; ¿Tú piensas continuar tus estudios en la Universidad?*
- forming the future tense of regular verbs by adding *-é, -ás, -á, -emos, -éis, -án* to the infinitive form: *estudiaré, comeremos, vivirán*
- forming the future tense of irregular verbs: *iré, haremos, dirán*
- forming the conditional tense using the future stem and imperfect endings *-ía, -ías, -ía, -íamos, -íais, ían* and using it to refer to what would happen or what you would do: *yo que tú iría en barco; sería difícil hacerlo en seguida; dijo que lo haría*
- using negative words before and after the verb: *nada, nadie, nunca, tampoco, ni ... ni*

Translate into Spanish

1 Spain intends to stay in the European Union for now.
2 Soon we will all be buying things online.
3 It would be a good idea to start learning more about computing now.
4 If I were you I would not allow my child free access to such websites.
5 Medical advances will help cure diseases in the developing world.
6 Why don't we think about the harm we are going to cause to the planet?
7 We would all like to have a perfect world.
8 It could be easy but no one is willing to make the effort.
9 It would be great if GM crops could solve the food crisis.
10 Nothing has ever stopped scientists from making progress.

1 España tiene la intención de quedarse en la Unión Europea por ahora.
2 Pronto todos compraremos cosas en línea.
3 Sería buena idea comenzar a aprender más sobre informática ahora.
4 Yo que tú no dejaría a mi hijo entrar en esos sitios web libremente.
5 Los avances médicos ayudarán a curar enfermedades de los países en desarrollo.
6 ¿Por qué no pensamos en el daño que vamos a causar al planeta?
7 A todos nos gustaría tener un mundo perfecto.
8 Podría ser fácil pero nadie quiere esforzarse.
9 Sería estupendo que los alimentos transgénicos pudieran resolver la crisis alimentaria.
10 Nada ha impedido jamás que los científicos realicen avances.

Revision of AS Grammar: past tenses – the preterite, imperfect and past continuous

Check the grammar section of Ánimo 2 and/or the Grammar Workbook if you need to know more about any of these areas:

- forming and using the preterite tense of regular and irregular verbs: *compré, comí, viví, hice, dije, puse, tuve, fui, estuve, hubo* etc.
- radical-changing verbs and when their spelling changes in the preterite tense: *saqué, jugué, empecé, creyó, murió, durmió, pidió, sintió* etc.
- forming and using the imperfect tense of regular and irregular verbs: *había, jugaba, comía, vivía, era, veía*
- the imperfect tense in time clauses in the past: *hacía cinco años que vivía allí*
- when to use the preterite and imperfect tenses: *fue / era, hubo / había*
- forming and using the past continuous to show interrupted action: *estaba durmiendo cuando la casa se incendió*

Translate into Spanish

1 How did we live before there were computers?
2 We would listen to the radio and chat to each other.
3 My grandmother used to go shopping nearly every day.
4 She even used to make her own bread if she had time.
5 We had lived in that house for seven years when Grandad died.
6 We were polluting the planet even then, all those years ago.
7 Coal-fired power stations made so much dirty smoke.
8 What were you doing when the first man landed on the moon?
9 A lot of people didn't believe what was happening.
10 Later everyone asked lots of questions about it.

1 ¿Cómo vivíamos antes de que existieran los ordenadores?
2 Escuchábamos la radio y charlábamos.
3 Mi abuela solía hacer las compras casi todos los días.
4 Hasta hacía su propio pan si tenía tiempo.
5 Hacía siete años que vivíamos en esa casa cuando murió el abuelo.
6 Aun entonces, hace muchos años, estábamos contaminando el planeta.
7 Las centrales de carbón produjeron mucho humo sucio.
8 ¿Qué estabas haciendo cuando aterrizó el primer hombre en la luna?
9 Mucha gente no creyó lo que estaba pasando.
10 Más tarde todos hicieron muchas preguntas acerca de eso.

Revision of AS Grammar: compound tenses in the past

Check the grammar section of Ánimo 2 and/or the Grammar Workbook if you need to know more about any of these areas:

- forming and using the perfect tense of regular verbs and all irregular past participles: *he, has, ha, hemos, habéis, han jugado / comido / vivido / escrito / dicho / puesto*
- forming and using reflexive verbs in the perfect tense: *se ha levantado tarde; ¿a qué hora te has acostado anoche?*
- the pluperfect tense: *había jugado; habías comido; habían vivido; había escrito*
- the perfect participle: *después de haber hecho esto; habiendo terminado; de haberlo sabido*

Translate into Spanish

1 Before transferring to Barcelona he had played for Sevilla.
2 He had wanted to play for Milan but they wouldn't pay him enough.
3 Having won all three medals there was nothing more to play for.
4 If only we had known this before we arrived.
5 I have written to my teacher again because he hasn't replied to my first letter.
6 After having gone to bed last night I remembered I hadn't put the cat out.
7 How many new states have joined the EU recently?
8 She said she didn't remember what had happened.
9 I would like to have finished it before this weekend.
10 I have never had enough time or money to do half the things I would have liked to do.

1 Antes de irse al Barcelona había jugado en el Sevilla.
2 Le hubiera gustado jugar para el Milán, pero no le pagaban lo suficiente.
3 Una vez que había ganado las tres medallas, no le quedaba más por lo que jugar.
4 Ojalá lo hubiéramos sabido antes de llegar.
5 He escrito a mi profesor otra vez porque no ha contestado a mi primera carta.
6 Después de haberme acostado anoche me acordé de que no había sacado al gato.
7 ¿Cuántos estados nuevos se han adherido a la Unión Europea recientemente?
8 Dijo que no recordaba lo que había pasado.
9 Me gustaría haberlo terminado antes de este fin de semana.
10 Nunca he tenido suficiente tiempo ni dinero para hacer ni la mitad de las cosas que me habría gustado hacer.

Revision of AS Grammar: the subjunctive including the imperative forms

The subjunctive mood is used when there are two different clauses in a sentence and the subject of one verb influences the other.

Check the grammar section of Ánimo 2 and/or the Grammar Workbook if you need to know more about any of these areas:

- how to form the subjunctive in the present and imperfect tenses
- using the subjunctive
- after verbs of wanting, requesting and advising: *quiero que hagas esto; me aconsejó que no lo hiciera*
- after verbs giving value judgements and expressing emotion: *es una lástima que ...; me sorprende que ...; es increíble que ...*
- after verbs expressing doubt or possibility: *dudaba que fuera verdad; puede ser que venga mañana*
- after impersonal expressions with adjectives: *es importante que; es imprescindible que ...*
- after *cuando* and other expressions of time when referring to the future: *cuando lo sepas dímelo; en cuanto vengas te lo explicaré*
- for polite commands – *usted / ustedes* – and **all** negative commands

Translate into Spanish

1. I am happy that my country is part of the European Union.
2. We are angry that the cost of living has gone up so much.
3. It is vital that we teach our children to recycle rubbish.
4. If we go on like this it's possible they won't have a happy future.
5. When they are grown up the world will be a very different place.
6. Please understand that this is not an idle threat.
7. They begged us to respect the environment.
8. Please don't throw your litter all over the mountainside.
9. I am so sorry that they have never appreciated the problem.
10. I have told you so many times not to do that.

1. Estoy contento de que mi país sea parte de la Unión Europea.
2. Nos enfurece que el coste de la vida haya subido tanto.
3. Es imprescindible que enseñemos a nuestros hijos a reciclar la basura.
4. Si seguimos así es posible que no tengan un futuro feliz.
5. Cuando sean mayores el mundo será un lugar muy diferente.
6. Por favor comprendan que esto va en serio.
7. Nos rogaron que respetáramos el medio ambiente.
8. Por favor no arrojen basura por toda la montaña.
9. Siento mucho que nunca hayan comprendido el problema.
10. Te he dicho repetidas veces que no hagas eso.

A2 Grammar: more about the subjunctive

What you need to know

- How to form the compound tenses of the subjunctive: *haya vuelto; hubiera querido*
- The subjunctive is also used ...
- after expressions of purpose: *para que; a fin de que*
- after expressions referring to concessions or conditions: *con tal de que; a menos que*
- in clauses describing a hypothetical or indefinite noun: *buscamos a una persona que pueda ayudarnos*
- in main clauses after
  ojalá: ojalá haga sol mañana
  tal vez / quizás: quizás vaya a llover más tarde
  como si: como si fuera tanto
  aunque meaning 'even if ...' but not 'although ...': *aunque fuera a llover*
- in set phrases: *sea como sea; digan lo que digan; pase lo que pase*
- after words ending in *-quiera* (-ever): *cualquiera, dondequiera*
- after *si* when used in past tense clauses which express a sense that the action is impossible or doubtful: *si hiciera esto ...; si lo hubiera sabido*
- Don't forget that when you make a sentence negative this often gives it an element of doubt; compare: *Creo que llegarán a tiempo* with *No creo que lleguen a tiempo.*

Translate into Spanish

1 Perhaps we won't ever see an end to terrorism.
2 There will always be a threat to world peace unless we can resolve these conflicts.
3 They doubted that the concert would have raised many funds.
4 I don't think he'll be punished even if he is proven guilty.
5 If only we could find a definite solution to end such poverty.
6 We've been looking for someone to help us sort this problem out.
7 It doesn't matter who so long as they are prepared to work hard.
8 I'm not sure he has enough patience for this type of work.
9 They treated him as if he were a criminal.
10 Wherever you live there will always be some racist attitudes.

1 Tal vez no veamos nunca el fin del terrorismo.
2 Seguirá existiendo una amenaza a la paz mundial a menos que resolvamos estos conflictos.
3 Dudaron que el concierto hubiera recaudado muchos fondos.
4 No creo que sea castigado aunque se le demuestre culpable.
5 Ojalá pudiéramos encontrar una solución definitiva para poner fin a tanta miseria.
6 Hemos estado buscando a alguien que pueda ayudarnos a resolver este problema.
7 No importa quien sea con tal de que esté dispuesto a trabajar duro.
8 No estoy seguro de que tenga suficiente paciencia para este tipo de trabajo.
9 Le trataron como si fuera un criminal.
10 Dondequiera que vivas siempre habrá actitudes racistas.

A2 Grammar: more complex tenses

What you need to know

At A2 Level you are expected to be familiar with the following more complex tenses.

- the future perfect:
  ¡Habré terminado en dos minutos! I will have finished in two minutes!
- the conditional perfect:
  Habría terminado antes pero no vi la hora. I would have finished sooner but I didn't see the time.
- the passive voice in all tenses – don't forget that the past participle must agree:
  Tu chaqueta estará terminada el lunes. Your jacket will be finished on Monday.
  Ha sido reparada por Juan. It has been repaired by Juan.
  Estaba siendo reparada por Miguel. It was being repaired by Miguel.
  Fue rota cuando la cojí en un gancho. It was torn when I caught it on a hook.
- Don't forget that you can often avoid the passive in Spanish by using either a reflexive form or an active form of the main verb:
  Terminaremos tu chaqueta el lunes. We will finish you jacket on Monday.
  Juan la ha reparado. Juan has repaired it.
  Miguel la estaba reparando. Miguel was repairing it.
  La rompí cuando la cojí en un gancho. I tore it when I caught it on a hook.
- dependent infinitives, such as *hacer reparar:*
  Manda a hacerla reparar. Send it to be repaired / have it repaired.
  Hágale entrar. Have him shown in.

Translate into Spanish

1 By 2050 life will have changed a great deal.
2 They will have invented an alternative source of fuel.
3 Will you have recycled everything?
4 She won't have learnt how to use it.
5 You would have liked Almodóvar's latest film.
6 Young criminals would have been locked up years ago.
7 How long will the euro have been in circulation?
8 Can you change this for me?
9 I thought it had already been changed.
10 It was damaged in an accident.

1 De aquí al año 2050 la vida habrá cambiado mucho.
2 Habrán inventado una fuente alternativa de fuel.
3 ¿Habrás reciclado todo?
4 No habrá aprendido a usarlo.
5 Te habría gustado la última película de Almodóvar.
6 Los delincuentes juveniles habrían sido encarcelados años atrás.
7 ¿Cuánto tiempo habrá estado en circulación el euro?
8 ¿Me lo puedes cambiar?
9 Pensé que ya había sido cambiado.
10 Fue dañado en un accidente.

- When you are speaking Spanish try to imagine yourself as a Spanish person.
- Read aloud to get used to the sound of your own voice in Spanish.
- Practise the sounds in front of a mirror – it helps if you can see the way your mouth moves to produce the different sounds.
- Record a simple song or an advert and imitate it.
- Practise asking questions then answering them yourself.
- Beware of reverting to an English accent when you see a word in Spanish which looks like an English word: *televisión* / television.
- Make sure you know how to say the alphabet in Spanish in order to spell out words.

The Spanish alphabet: listen to the sounds and repeat them. (Track 8)
A B C D E F G ... H I J K L M ... N Ñ O P Q R ... S T U V W ... X Y Z
It helps to learn them in groups. Sing them to one of your favourite tunes. Note: *Ññ* is a separate letter in Spanish and comes after *N* in alphabetical lists. All the letters are feminine.

The vowel sounds
Spanish vowels are always clearly pronounced and not relaxed in unstressed syllables as happens in English. **Listen and practise the vowels. (Track 9)**
Alba Arbalaez abre su abanico amarillo amablemente.
Enrique Esquivel escoge el edredón más elegante.
Inés Iglesias indica que es imposible ingresar allí.
Óscar Ordóñez odia las hojas otoñales.
Umberto Umbral usa un uniforme ultramoderno.

Consonants
Spanish *g* is pronounced hard as in '**g**ate' before *a*, *o* or *u* and soft like an exaggerated English 'h' before *e* and *i*.
Spanish *c* is pronounced hard as in '**c**ow' before *a*, *o* or *u* and soft as in '**th**ing' before *e* and *i*.

3 Practise these sounds. (Track 10)
hard *c*: *caballo, conejo, culebra*
soft *c* : *cero, cisne*
hard *g* : *gato, gorila, gusano*
soft *g* : *gente, gimnasta*

Some spellings change to preserve the sounds:
The hard *c* sound as in '**c**ow' is written *qu* before *e* or *i*: *sacar* but *sa**qu**é*
The hard *g* sound as in '**g**ate' is written *gu* before *e* or *i*: *pagar* but *pa**gu**é*
The soft *c* sound as in '**th**ing' is written *z* before *a* or *o*: *empecé* but *empezar*
The soft *g* sound like an exaggerated English 'h' is written *j* before *a* or *o*: *coger* but *cojo*
The sound *gu* as in '**gu**ava' is written *gü* before *e* or *i*: *averi**gu**ar* but *averi**güé***

The position of a consonant in the word also affects its sound: a consonant at the beginning of a word is usually pronounced harder than in the middle or at the end.

La letra d: (Track 11)
donde *adonde*
dámelo *me lo ha dado*
drogas *cuidado*

La letra ll:
llegar *Sevilla*

La letra r:
revista *pero*

La letra s:
sí me gustan las tapas
suelen ser muy malas

La letra x:
exacto *taxi, texto*

Try to read out the following tongue-twisters. Compare your pronunciation with the recording. (Track 12)

Es verdad que la ventana verde está en Madrid.
Llora la llama cuando llueve. Que no llore la llama cuando llueva.
Jorge juega ajedrez. Jugando ajedrez Jorge juró jugar con justicia.

r* and *rr

Listen to the difference between the words *pero* and *perro*. If you have problems with this sound in Spanish, listen and practise it as much as you can. (Track 13)

The letter *r* sounds softer in the middle of a word – *pero, Pedro* – and harder at the beginning of a word: *revista, Roberto*

Double *rr* sounds strongest:
Llora la guitarra con rabia y dulzura.
El perro comió una pera. Pero la perra no comió el peral.

Once you have mastered all the different sounds you need to make sure you are confident about where to place the stress on each word.

Here is the basic rule:

In words which end in a vowel, *s* or *n* the spoken stress falls naturally on the second to last syllable: *instrum**e**nto, import**a**ntes, repres**e**ntan.*

In words which end in a consonant (except *s* or *n*) the stress falls naturally on the last syllable: *anim**a**l, alreded**o**r, nar**i**z.*

All words which do **not** follow this rule require a written accent to indicate where the spoken stress falls: *última, histórico, tecnología*.

Spoken stress and vowels

For the purposes of stress *a*, *e* and *o* are considered to be 'strong' vowels, and *i* and *u* are considered 'weak'.

- If the spoken stress falls on a syllable containing two vowels then the stronger one is stressed: *oficial* (pronounced *ofici**a**l not ofic**i**al*).
- If both are strong vowels, they are considered to be separate syllables: *levantaos* (pronounced *levant**a**os*).
- If both are weak vowels then the stress falls on the second one: *cuida* (pronounced *cu**i**da* not *c**u**ida*).
- If the word does **not** follow these rules then the stress is marked by a written accent: *país, queríamos*.

Finally, having practised all these individual sounds, you need to make sure the whole sentence sounds Spanish.

Intonation (Track 14)
Your voice should rise and fall when you speak.
In Spanish it should fall:

- at the end of a short sentence. *Toco la guitarra.* (I play the guitar.)

It should rise:

- at the end of another type of question: *¿Tienes una flauta?* (Have you got a flute?)
- in the middle of longer sentences: *Tú tienes una flauta y yo tengo una guitarra.* (You've got a flute and I've got a guitar.)

***Sinalefa* and *entrelazamiento* (Track 15)**

In spoken Spanish, vowel sounds and consonants slide into each other, which helps to make the sentence flow.
When vowel sounds end and begin consecutive words they are linked together. This is known as ***sinalefa***.
A final consonant is linked together with a following vowel. This is known as ***entrelazamiento***.

1 Copy these words and phrases and indicate the *sinalefa* and *entrelazamiento*.

2 Listen to these verses and try to imitate the pronunciation.

El otoño: isla
de perfil estricto
que pone en olvido
la onda indecisa.

¡Amor a la línea!
La vid se desnuda
de una vestidura
demasiado rica.

¡Oh claridad! Pía
tanto entre las hojas
que quieren ser todas
a un tiempo amarillas.

¡Trabazón de brisas
entre cielo y álamo!
Y todo el espacio,
tan continuo, vibra.

Esta luz antigua
de tarde feliz
no puede morir.
¡Ya es mía, ya es mía!

Unit 1 – La energía y la contaminación

la contaminación	*pollution*
generar	*to generate / create*
la calefacción	*heating*
los residuos	*waste*
el vertedero	*rubbish dump*
enterrar	*to submerge / bury*
emitir	*to emit / give off*
verter	*to spill / pour away*
la sequía	*drought*
la desertificación	*desertification*
químico/a	*chemical*
escalofriante	*staggering / mind-blowing*
la energía eólica	*wind energy*
los aerogeneradores	*wind turbines*
las hélices	*turbines / propellers*
fotovoltaico/a	*solar*
invernadero	*greenhouse*
un derroche	*a waste*
el calentamiento global	*global warming*
costear el lujo	*to afford*
empeñarse en	*to be determined*
atascado/a	*blocked up*
concienciar	*to make aware*
la desaceleración	*slowing down*
contundente	*overwhelming*
el auge	*boom*
el desplome	*nosedive*
frenar	*to brake / put a stop to*
incrementar	*to increase*
rechazar	*to reject*
inocuo/a	*harmless*
dañino/a	*harmful*
el riesgo	*risk*
agotar	*to run out of*
la huella de carbono	*carbon footprint*
vedar	*to ban, prohibit*

Unit 2 – ¡SOS Protejamos nuestro planeta!

el entorno	*surroundings / environs*
transgénico/a	*GM (crops)*
amenazar	*to threaten*
la cadena	*chain*
la deforestación	*deforestation*
el propósito	*purpose / reason*
desperdiciar	*to waste*
aprovechar	*to take advantage of / maximise*
las materias primas	*raw materials*
la degradación	*spoiling / decomposition*
las latas	*tins*
envases tipo brick	*cartons*
vidrio	*glass*
provisto	*provided*
el veredicto	*verdict*
quejarse	*to complain*
abordar	*to tackle / deal with*
sensato/a	*sensible*
el desplazamiento	*displacement*
las emisiones	*exhaust*
medio	*average*
un ahorro	*a saving*
yendo a	*going to*
apoyar	*to support*
el impacto paisajístico	*impact on the countryside*
las vías ferroviarias	*railways*
el deterioro	*deterioration*
caber	*to fit in*
el crecimiento	*increase*
desmesurado/a	*enormous / excessive*
los umbrales	*threshold*
la alfabetización	*literacy*
cotidiano/a	*daily*
abastecer	*to provide*
nocivo/a	*harmful*

Unit 3 – Tierras cosmopólitas

acoger	*to welcome*
de acogida	*reception*
el rechazo	*rejection*
prejuicio	*prejudice*
la convivencia	*coexistence*
el asilo	*asylum*
la inmigración	*immigration*
huir	*to flee*
la incertidumbre	*uncertainty*
adinerado/a	*wealthy*
sobrevivir	*to survive*
la osadía	*daring*
intentar	*to attempt to*
imprevisto/a	*unforeseen*
el fracaso	*failure*
la plantilla laboral	*workforce*
la vivienda	*housing*
el matadero	*slaughterhouse*
mezclarse	*to mix*
atraer	*to attract*
alquilar	*to hire*
el gueto	*ghetto*
desacato/a	*contempt / disobeying*
ajustar	*to adjust*
salvaguardar	*to safeguard*
una patera	*raft*
forastero/a	*foreign*
carecer de	*to lack*
brindar	*to offer*
el capataz	*foreman*
la discapacidad	*disability*
las chabolas	*shanty town / shacks*
aguantar	*to put up with*
encarcelar	*to imprison*
un temporero	*temporary worker*
denunciar	*to denounce*
empadronar	*to register (with authorities)*

Unit 4 – La riqueza y la pobreza

la riqueza	*wealth*
la pobreza	*poverty*
prestigioso/a	*famous / renowned*
el terreno	*land*
el ingreso	*income*
el sueldo medio	*average wage*
un tercio	*a third*
la tasa de	*rate of*
enriquecerse	*to get rich*
empobrecerse	*to become poor*
el comercio libre	*free trade*
el consumismo	*consumerism*
las tarifas	*taxes / tariffs*
los subsidios	*subsidies*
un dineral	*a vast amount of money*
dar de comer a	*to feed*
el microcrédito	*microcredit*
invertir	*to invest*
prestar	*to lend*
criar	*to rear*
la cabra	*goat*
conllevar	*to bring with*
pudiendo	*being able to*
el presupuesto	*budget*
mudo/a	*dumb*
divergente	*opposite*
mejorar	*to make better*
sin afán de lucro	*without interest*
fomentar	*to encourage*
un diputado	*a member of parliament*
desafiar	*to challenge*
las subvenciones	*subsidies*
la empresa	*company*
superarse	*to improve oneself*

Unit 5 – El crimen y el castigo

el castigo	*punishment*
el delito	*offence / crime*
las pandillas	*gangs*
la cárcel	*prison*
el recluso	*prisoner*
la fianza	*bail*
culpable	*guilty*
un abogado	*a lawyer*
la ciencia forense	*forensic science*
una anciana	*an old lady*
en el punto de mira	*(to have) in one's sights / one's eyes on*
vinculado/a	*linked to*
reprimir	*to repress*
la riña	*brawl / fight*
equivocado/a	*mistaken*
la red	*a network*
apoyar	*to help / back up*
aliarse	*to get together*
luchar	*to struggle / fight*
el lastre	*burden / might / full force*
el malhechor	*evildoer / wicked person*
una celda	*a cell*
aliviarse	*to alleviate / make better*
el narcotraficante	*drugs trafficker*
despreciar	*to despise*
las pautas	*guidelines / criteria*
alegar	*to allege*
tramitar	*to deal with*
comparecer ante	*to appear before / be judged by*
las cortes	*court*
atracar	*to assault / mug*
el desempleo	*unemployment*
los derechos	*rights*
detener	*to detain*

Unit 6 – Avances científicos, médicos y tecnológicos

los avances	*advances*
la clonación	*cloning*
el ADN	*DNA*
los OGM	*GMO's*
la nanotecnología	*nanotechnology*
la reproducción asistida	*IVF*
las prótesis	*prosthetics*
el ordenador	*computer*
el portal	*webpage / portal*
el ratón	*mouse*
potente	*powerful*
capaz de	*capable of*
la cirugía	*surgery*
el tejido	*tissue*
indeseado/a	*undesirable*
el tamaño	*size*
afrontar	*to confront / face up to*
sobrepesar	*to outweigh*
discapacitado/a	*disabled*
el trasplante	*transplant*
una célula	*a cell*
el rechazo	*rejection*
la escasez	*scarcity*
descubrir	*to discover*
el descubrimiento	*discovery*
la compra en línea	*online shopping*
el desarrollo	*development*
la carrera espacial	*space race*
las misiones espaciales	*space missions*
el artilugio	*artefact / gadget*
puntero/a	*at the forefront*
ingenioso/a	*ingenious / clever*
el dispositivo	*gadget*
una sonda	*space probe*
el hallazgo	*finding / discovery*
respaldar	*to back up*
una herramienta	*tool*
los internautas	*Internet users*

Unit 7 – Talento hispano

los artes	*arts*
las artes visuales	*visual arts*
la escultura	*sculpture*
la lengua	*language / tongue*
ambientarse	*to take place*
pretender	*to try to*
la meta	*aim*
la palabra escrita	*written word*
las dotes	*gifts / talents*
una afición	*a hobby*
el estreno	*debut / first showing / premier*
el espectador	*spectator*
sorprender	*to surprise*
destacar	*to stand out*
hacer burla de	*to make fun of*
entretenido/a	*entertaining*
desconcertante	*disconcerting / upsetting*
la pantalla	*screen*
la rebeldía	*rebelliousness*
los modales	*manners*
el orfanato	*orphanage*
arrasar	*to take by storm*
pegadizo/a	*catchy*
sin pudor	*no decency*
escandalizarse	*to scandalise*
enfurecerse	*to make furious*
un espectáculo	*a show*
las palmas	*palms (of hand)*
los tacones	*heels (of shoe)*
el remordimiento	*remorse*
el destino	*destiny*
arrepentirse	*to repent*

Unit 8 – Patrimonio e historia

el patrimonio	*heritage*
el auge	*rise*
el ocaso	*fall*
el crisol	*melting pot*
las tinieblas	*dark ages*
la fe	*faith / religion*
asolar	*to lay waste / ravage*
la dictadura	*dictatorship*
la derrota	*defeat*
lograr	*to succeed in*
desvanecer	*to fade*
indígenos	*native*
los inmigrantes	*immigrants*
independizarse	*to become independent*
el apodo	*nickname*
bilingüe	*bilingual*
gratis	*for free*
agradecido/a	*thankful*
una nueva ola	*a new wave*
la población	*population*
la plata	*silver*
el estaño	*tin*
la lucha	*struggle*
cruento/a	*bloody*
los hitos	*milestones / landmarks*
la cámera	*chamber (as in government)*
el sindicato	*union of workers*
aprobar	*to approve / pass a law*
una herida	*wound*
el rehén	*hostage*
adolorido/a	*upset / hurt*
la soberanía	*sovereignty*
entregarse	*to hand over / give in*
borrar	*to rub out / erase*
la tasa de natalidad	*birthrate*

Unit 9 – Política y polémicas globales

gobernar / el gobierno	*to govern / government*
la hambruna	*famine / hunger*
la deuda	*debt*
las pandemias	*pandemics*
acercar	*to approach / draw near*
la desigualdad	*inequality*
audaz	*daring*
innegable	*undeniable*
dictaminar	*to dictate*
autogobierno	*self-rule*
los arquetipos	*stereotypes*
el colmo	*limit*
respaldar	*to back up*
la mili	*military service*
la botellona	*binge drinking*
culpar	*to blame*
un juicio	*a trial*
un régimen	*a regime (government)*
un intercambio	*an exchange*
radicar	*to have roots*
el comportamiento	*behaviour*
el poder	*power*
el lema	*slogan*
manifestar	*to protest*
la campaña	*campaign*
apelar	*to appeal to*
los asesinos	*assassins*
disfrazarse	*to disguise oneself*
matar / la matanza	*to kill / killing*
dispares	*disparate*
alcanzar	*to achieve / reach*
fracasar / un fracaso	*to fail / failure*
amenazar	*to threaten*
entrometerse	*to meddle*
un juez	*a judge*

Answers to tasks

Listening task 1

a) ~~ha contado~~; cuenta con

b) ~~poco más de la mitad~~; el 45%

c) ~~los abuelos los~~; las abuelas las

d) ~~gozar~~; olvidarse

Listening task 2

a) C; b) E; c) A; d) G; e) F

Listening task 3

Verdad: c); e); f); i); j)

Listening task 4

a) C; b) A; c) A

Reading task 1

a) personas; b) bases; c) lema; d) soldado; e) manifestantes; f) tropas; g) formaciones; h) paz; i) imperialismo; j) tiempo

Reading task 2

a) N; b) V; c) F; d) N; e) F; f) V

Reading and Writing task 3

A child phenomenon

At twenty three years old, Mark Zuckerberg has become one of the most influential people in the world thanks to the creation of Facebook. The site already has more than 64 million users who share their opinions and likes and dislikes with their friends. Who was that genius who when he was only 19 years old created this Internet monster?

Already in his second year at Harvard he almost got himself expelled because of his pranks as a hacker. He created Facesmash, a webpage where university students could match up couples and vote for the most attractive in the faculty. It was a huge success. From then on he became obsessed with the idea of creating a social networking site.

Reading and Writing task 4

a) Tras meses de muy poca lluvia Cataluña ha tenido que pedir ayuda a Madrid.

b) Sin embargo, es dudoso que puedan resolver el problema rápidamente.

c) El país está luchando por resolver la peor sequía en cuarenta años.

d) Cataluña, en el noreste, ha sido gravemente afectada.

e) Las autoridades de Barcelona van a multar a la gente por regar el jardín.

f) No se permite a nadie llenar una piscina de más de 300 metros cuadrados.

g) Las fuentes han sido vaciadas y las duchas de la playa cerradas.

infinitive	present	preterite	imperfect	future	conditional	present subjunctive	imperfect subjunctive	present participle	past participle
comprar	*compro*	*compré*	*compraba*	*compraré*	*compraría*	*compre*	*comprara/se*	*comprando*	*comprado*
to buy	**I** buy	**I** bought	**I** used to buy	**I** will buy	**I** would buy	buy	bought	buying	bought
comer	*como*	*comí*	*comía*	*comeré*	*comería*	*coma*	*comiera/se*	*comiendo*	*comido*
subir	*subo*	*subí*	*subía*	*subiré*	*subiría*	*suba*	*subiera/se*	*subiendo*	*subido*
levantarse	*me levanto*	*me levanté*	*me levantaba*	*me levantaré*	*me levantaría*	*me levante*	*me levantara/se*	*levantándome*	*levantado*
dar	*doy*	*di*	*daba*	*daré*	*daría*	*dé*	*diera/se*	*dando*	*dado*
decir	*digo*	*dije*	*decía*	*diré*	*diría*	*diga*	*dijera/se*	*diciendo*	*dicho*
estar	*estoy*	*estuve*	*estaba*	*estaré*	*estaría*	*esté*	*estuviera/se*	*estando*	*estado*
haber	*he*	*hube*	*había*	*habré*	*habría*	*haya*	*hubiera/se*	*habiendo*	*habido*
hacer	*hago*	*hice*	*hacía*	*haré*	*haría*	*haga*	*hiciera/se*	*haciendo*	*hecho*
ir	*voy*	*fui*	*iba*	*iré*	*iría*	*vaya*	*fuera/se*	*yendo*	*ido*
poder	*puedo*	*pude*	*podía*	*podré*	*podría*	*pueda*	*pudiera/se*	*pudiendo*	*podido*
poner	*pongo*	*puse*	*ponía*	*pondré*	*pondría*	*ponga*	*pusiera/se*	*poniendo*	*puesto*
querer	*quiero*	*quise*	*quería*	*querré*	*querría*	*quiera*	*quisiera/se*	*queriendo*	*querido*
saber	*sé*	*supe*	*sabía*	*sabré*	*sabría*	*sepa*	*supiera/se*	*sabiendo*	*sabido*
ser	*soy*	*fui*	*era*	*seré*	*sería*	*sea*	*fuera/se*	*siendo*	*sido*
tener	*tengo*	*tuve*	*tenía*	*tendré*	*tendría*	*tenga*	*tuviera/se*	*teniendo*	*tenido*
traer	*traigo*	*traje*	*traía*	*traeré*	*traería*	*traiga*	*trajera/se*	*trayendo*	*traído*
venir	*vengo*	*vine*	*venía*	*vendré*	*vendría*	*venga*	*viniera/se*	*viniendo*	*venido*